Problems in Philosophy

PERCEPTION

Godfrey Vesey read Moral Science at Cambridge in 1947–50, and became lecturer and then reader in philosophy at the University of London. He has contributed articles to *Essays in Philosophical Psychology* (1964), *Perceiving, Sensing, and Knowing* (1965), *The Concept of Education* (1967), *The Human Agent* (1968), *Mill* (1968), among others, and is the author of *The Embodied Mind* (1965). He has been Director of the Royal Institute of Philosophy since 1966. His present work as Professor of Philosophy at The Open University, Bletchley, England, involves him in teaching philosophy by B.B.C. radio and television.

PERCEPTION

GODFREY VESEY

ANCHOR BOOKS
Doubleday & Company, Inc.
Garden City, New York
1971

Anchor Books edition: 1971

Library of Congress Catalog Card Number 70–144311
Copyright © 1971 by G. N. A. Vesey
All Rights Reserved
Printed in the United States of America
First Edition

CONTENTS

CONTENTS

PREFACE

It has been supposed that there is a problem, of the "how do we, how can we, know?" variety, about what we would ordinarily say we perceive. For some reason it has been thought that the fact that we can misperceive things means that *all* perception is suspect, that what we say, even when we have not misperceived, is in need of some sort of standing justification. This will be a familiar story to anyone who has researched in the recent philosophical literature on perception. First the reader's attention is drawn to the possibility of illusion. Then it is argued that our everyday talk—the whole "language game," as a Wittgensteinian would say—is off the mark as regards the objects of perception. What we are really aware of, in perception as in misperception, are "sense-data," "sensations," "impressions," or "appearances." If our everyday talk is to be saved, the philosopher must show that it is related in a thoroughly proper way to what might be said in the sense-datum, etc., language. His task is that of *analyzing* "physical object statements" in terms of statements about sense-data, sensations, impressions, or appearances.

This, I say, is a familiar story. Some philosophers are still at it, adding new chapters or, more probably, regurgitating old ones. For the most part they manage to avoid skepticism and idealism, and end up reasonably satisfied that they have saved the world for mankind—although the world may have become a less substantial, or a less colorful, place in the process.

Other philosophers, an increasing number, are busy digging the ground from under the feet of the first ones. They are engaged in showing that the start of the story is really a non-starter. Incorrect perception is intelligible only if there is the possibility of correct perception. And so any attempt to disestablish our everyday talk is broken-backed from the start.

Worthwhile though it might be systematically to expound and examine the arguments for and against the bankruptcy of the physical object language, I think that at this stage of the game there is a fresher and more exciting task. It is that of trying to understand the climate of thought in which the argument from illusion flourished. In particular, how is it that the argument found such a ready response? Why were people so ready with alternative "objects of perception" to those underwritten by the physical object language?

If there is one historically valid answer, it lies, I maintain, in people wanting to give a causal, or a partly causal, answer to a question about perception that is not causal. The question has traditionally been referred

to as that of the relation of appearance to reality, and
it is part of the climate of thought that it should not be
asked what the word "appearance" means in the
question.

Answers to questions beget further questions. Why
should people want to give a causal, or a partly causal,
answer to a question about perception that is not
causal? Part of the answer, I suggest, is because they
have accepted a causal, or a partly causal, answer to
another question, the question "What am I?" Their answer to the question "What am I?" is reflected in their
answer to the question "What is it for me to perceive
something?" The answer they have accepted to the
question "What am I?" is "A being distinct from all
physical objects in a sense of 'distinct' which means
that however closely I am connected with one particular physical object ('my' body), it is at best a causal
connection." On this answer to the question "What am
I?," my eyes become "my" eyes, that is, not literally a
part of me, and what I am aware of in perception is
"introjected" (to use Richard Avenarius's term) to become an "idea," "sensation," or "sense-impression,"
the effect of the senses being acted on by what is by
now "the external world."

Going back still further, we encounter the question
"Why have people accepted a partly causal answer to
the question 'What am I?'" One answer would be:
because they have been persuaded by Descartes's argu-

ment for this answer. The argument is on the following
lines:

> For me to think at all I must exist. Therefore, "I exist,"
> when I think it, is necessarily true. Therefore I cannot
> think "I exist," and doubt its truth. Therefore I have
> only to think "I exist" to be certain of its truth. There-
> fore inasmuch as I can think "I exist" I am certain that
> I exist. But at the same time as being certain that I
> exist, I can (because I might be dreaming, be deceived
> by an extremely powerful malicious demon, etc.) doubt
> that I have a body. Therefore insofar as I am certain of
> my existence I am no more than a thinking being.
> Therefore I can think of myself existing as simply a
> thinking being, that is, as a being distinct from a body.
> But God, being omnipotent, could have made me as I
> can think of myself, and if God could have made me as
> a being distinct from a body, then I really am distinct
> from a body. And the closest relation I can have with
> something distinct from myself is at best a causal rela-
> tion.

One could now try to answer the question "Why
have people been persuaded by this argument?" and it
would be interesting to do so; but one has to stop some-
where.

Plan of the book

I have referred to people wanting to give a causal, or a
partly causal, answer to a question about perception

that is not causal. My first task is to specify what that question is. Saying that it is the question of the relation of appearance to reality is not sufficient. The word "appears," or "looks like," is used in a variety of ways, and in one of them the relation of appearance to reality *is* causal (if the laws of perspective are causal laws). In Chapter 1 I try to make clear what the sense of "appearance" is with which I am concerned. I call it the "epistemic" appearance, to distinguish it from what I call the "optical" appearance and from the "resembles" sense of "looks like." I claim that perception would not be how we find things out about the world if there were not epistemic appearances.

In Chapter 2 I note, for future discussion, D. W. Hamlyn's answer to the question of the relation of appearance to reality, the answer which consists in saying that "the connection between the way people see coloured objects and what colours those objects actually have . . . lies in our concepts." I go on to consider the Cartesian answer to the question, in terms of (a) the physical object acting on the mind via the sense organs and brain to produce a "sense-impression" in the mind, (b) a thought about the sense-impression, and (c) a thought about the "external" object that causes the sense-impression. I consider how, in terms of his theory, Descartes deals with illusions, and then introduce three objections to his theory. The first—that the sense-impression is said to be a modification of a non-extended substance, the essence of which is thought, and yet *is* extended and is unlike a thought in that it is not true or false of anything—is dealt with by making the essence of the mind, not thinking (meaning, by "thinking," what can be true or false of something), but privacy.

In Chapter 3 I consider the second objection to Descartes's theory. This concerns the thought about the sense-impression which, on his theory, has to do duty for the thought that a physical object has a certain quality, such as whiteness. The implications of Descartes's theory are made plain in what J. S. Mill says on the subject in Book I of his *System of Logic*. In brief, Descartes is committed to just such a private language theory as Wittgenstein attacks in his *Philosophical Investigations*. Having made this plain, I have not thought fit to go on to add to the literature on private languages.

In Chapter 4 I examine the account Descartes gives of the relationship between having an idea (sense-impression) and thinking there is a cause of it external to the mind. What is significant about it is his admission that, except insofar as we may be able to establish that God would not make us strongly inclined to believe what was false, we have no means of establishing the origin of our ideas. Another way of putting this is to say that the sentence "Our ideas proceed from corporeal objects" does not mean anything to us in terms of any conceivable verifying experience. One way of giving it a meaning in such terms would be to *define* "ideas proceeding from corporeal objects" as "ideas which are attended with other ideas in a regular train or series." To this it might be objected that it would mean that physical objects come into and go out of existence as we have ideas of them. This could be avoided by bringing "possible ideas" into the definition. Then matter would be what Mill calls "a Permanent Possibility of Sensation." This is phenomenalism, acceptance of which would involve us in denying the logical compatibility of "All actual and possible sensations are such as to confirm the existence of a table in my study" and "There is not a table in my study." Their logical compatibility is, however, part of what we mean by a physical object.

In Chapter 5 I distinguish two meanings that may be given to the words "Are there physical objects?" In one they ask a question *within* the realm of physical objects; in the other, a question *about* the realm. As a question within the realm, the words merit a puzzled look, and "Of course," with the puzzled look predominating. The meaning I propose for the words "Are there physical objects?," so that they ask a question *about* the realm of physical objects, is one about the logical truths of the language relating how things appear and how things are. These logical truths are not such as to entail phenomenalism.

In Chapter 6, after recapitulating the argument of the preceding five chapters, I expound Hamlyn's argument for there being a conceptual connection "between the way people see coloured objects and what colour those objects actually have." The crux of the argument, as I understand it, is that the truth of "Red things normally look red to us" is involved in our having the concept *red;* it is necessarily true, not in the sense of being analytic ("is red" does not *mean* "looks red under normal conditions"), but in the sense of having to be true to be intelligible; there is this conceptual, but not analytic, connection between being red and looking red under normal conditions.

Notes, Bibliography and Index

At the end of the book are (i) Notes on Reading, (ii) Bibliography, and (iii) Index. The quantity of philosophical work on perception is such as to make any attempt at an inclusive bibliography out of the question. I have listed only the works referred to in the text and in the notes on reading.

PERCEPTION

1

THE EPISTEMIC APPEARANCE

G. E. M. Anscombe (2)* tells of a man out shooting who misperceived his father as a stag, with fatal consequences. What the huntsman was looking at was, in fact, his father; but his father looked to him like a stag, and, thinking that he was shooting a stag, the huntsman shot his father.

Faced with such a situation, philosophers, unlike doctors and policemen, ask such questions as: "Are there two uses, or senses, of 'see,' in one of which the huntsman saw his father, and in the other of which he saw a stag?" "Are there two ways of seeing things, corresponding to these two uses of 'see'?" "Are there two different kinds of object of sight, corresponding to the two ways of seeing things?"

One thing that might be said is that if, at the time, we had asked the huntsman what it was he saw moving in the undergrowth he would have said, "A stag," whereas if we had asked others with a better view what it was the huntsman's rifle was actually pointing at, they would have said, "His father." In that he misperceived his father as a stag, the huntsman was not aware that his rifle was pointing at his father and so would not have said that what he saw moving in the undergrowth was his father. This would seem to cover the

* Numerals in parentheses refer to works numerically listed in the Bibliography on pp. 93–96.

situation without committing us to saying that there are, or are not, different senses of "see," different ways of seeing, or different kinds of object of sight. Let us not commit ourselves to more than we need for the purpose in hand.

One of the phrases used in the initial description of the situation was, ". . . his father looked to him like a stag. . . ." It was then said that if at the time we had asked the huntsman what it was he saw moving he would have said, "A stag."

Is it the case that whenever we talk of an object looking like a such-and-such, or looking so-and-so, to someone, the person in question would say that what he saw was a such-and-such, or was so-and-so? No. Two classes of exceptions to this generalization are (i) that of visual illusions, such as the Muller-Lyer illusion; and (ii) that of cases in which, when we say something looked like a such-and-such to someone, we mean no more than that he noticed a resemblance.

(i) In the case of the Muller-Lyer illusion, I know

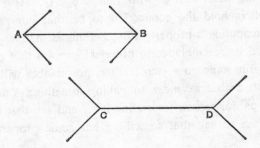

lines AB and CD to be equal in length, having meas-
ured them, but they still look unequal. That is, they
look unequal without my judging what I see to be in
fact unequal lines.

And (ii) I can say that my daughter looks like me
without implying that I mistake her for myself. I am
merely drawing attention to a resemblance. But when,
in Anscombe's story, his father looked to the huntsman like a stag, he *did* mistake him for one. If it had
merely been a matter of noticing a resemblance he
would not have shot him. One does not shoot one's
father just because he resembles a stag.

Are the two classes of exceptions really distinct
classes? Or, for example, when we say that the lines in
the Muller-Lyer figure look unequal do we mean that
they resemble unequal lines? A small green patch on a
large yellow background looks blue (the effect of color
contrast). In saying it looks blue do I simply mean
that it resembles blue things?

Many philosophers hold that there is a connection
between something's having some property and its resembling other things with that property. Most philosophers hold the connection to be that our *reason*
for attributing a property to something is that we have
noticed its resemblance to other things with that property. But some go a step further, presumably with the
idea that what we *mean* by calling something X is the
same as our *reason* for calling it X, and say that what
it *means* to say that something has some property is

that it resembles other things with that same property. R. M. Hare, for example, writes:

> One of the features of descriptive meaning . . . is that it relies upon the concept of similarity. . . . A descriptive meaning-rule is one which lays it down that we may apply an expression to objects which are similar to each other in certain respects. . . . Suppose that I say that *X* is red; I am committed to holding that anything which is like *X* in the relevant respect is also red. But suppose that I am asked what *is* the relevant respect. I shall be able to answer this question only by giving an indication, vague or precise, of what it was about *X* that made me call it red; i.e. by explaining what I meant by calling it red (20, Ch. 2, Sect. 3, p. 13).

I shall refer to these two views about the connection between something's having some property and its resembling other things with that property as the "reason" and "meaning" versions of "the resemblance doctrine." Hare could be represented as holding that the reason version is true, and that therefore the meaning version is true.

To the meaning version it might be objected that if to say that something is *X* is to say that it is like other things which are *X,* then the same analysis must be given of what it is to say that the other things are *X,* and we are involved in a vicious regress. Things can resemble one another only if they have some property in respect of which they resemble one another; resemblance is a consequential relation, and what it is consequential upon cannot be analyzed in terms of it.

In a paper published in 1950 (6), A. J. Ayer clearly distinguished between the reason version and the meaning version. He held the former but not the latter. His reason for not holding the latter was not that it involves a vicious regress, but that we could meaningfully say that something was green even if nothing else that was green actually existed. This objection, but not the objection that the meaning version involves a vicious regress, could be met by saying that the things which something, to be green, must resemble need only be imaginable. But perhaps this move would take away from the meaning version some of its attractiveness.

I think Ayer may have renounced even the reason version of the resemblance doctrine. In 1956 he wrote, "Except when a word is patently ambiguous, it is natural for us to assume that the different situations, or types of situation, to which it applies have a distinctive common feature. For otherwise why should we use the same word to refer to them?" (9, Ch. 1, Sect. 2)

In this quotation he gives the reason version of what might be called "the common property doctrine" as an argument for things which are X all having X in common. What I find puzzling is his use of the word "assume." What would it be to discover that the assumption that all green things have greenness in common was mistaken?

It is for the same reason that I find puzzling what Morris Lazerowitz says on the subject:

> The fact that there are no sharp lines of demarcation [between something being a horse and being a swan] shows that there is no property common and unique to all things, actual or imaginable, to which the word 'horse' is applicable and the failure to have which makes the word inapplicable. The meaning of the word is not an essence, a common property. . . . The *fact* with regard to abstract words is that they are applicable to each of a number of things because the things resemble each other more or less, without there being anything common to all of them to set exact boundaries which would mark off correct from incorrect application of the words (27, pp. 11–15).

Unlike Ayer, Lazerowitz does not explicitly distinguish between reason and meaning versions of the resemblance and common property doctrines. If the distinction *is* made, then I think he can be fairly represented as arguing from the truth of the reason version of the resemblance doctrine to the falsity of the meaning version of the common property doctrine. It is his use of the word *"fact"* (the italicization is his) which I find puzzling in the same way as Ayer's use of the word "assume." Its use suggests that he could understand what it would be for the reason version of the common property doctrine to be true, and can somehow see that it is never in fact true.

With regard to the meaning versions of the two doc-

trines, my own view is that the meaning version of the
resemblance doctrine is necessarily false, because it involves a vicious regress; and that the meaning version
of the common property doctrine is necessarily true—
but trivially so, because "these two things have a common property, X" means no more than that they are
both X.

With regard to the reason versions, I would contend
that the reason version of the resemblance doctrine
cannot be true in some cases unless it is false in others.
That is, unless it is sometimes the case that something
can be seen to have a property, X, then it can never be
the case that something else can be seen to be like it.
But my holding that the reason version of the resemblance doctrine must be false in some cases if it is to be
true in others does not commit me to holding that the
reason version of the common property doctrine must
be true in some cases. I say this not because I cannot
attach a meaning to the reason version of the common
property doctrine (though this is true), but because I
am persuaded by Wittgenstein's arguments in the second half of *The Brown Book,* that it is false that a person cannot use a word to describe something without
having some reason for applying it.

I conclude from this discussion of the resemblance
doctrine that when we say that the lines in the Muller-
Lyer figure look unequal in length, we do not necessarily mean that they resemble unequal lines. *Some
things must look X in a non-resemblance sense if any-*

thing is to look *X* in a resemblance sense, and, on the face of it, "The lines look unequal in length" does not resemble a typical resemblance use of "looks" such as "My daughter looks like me." It does not resemble it in this respect: that whereas one can be asked, "In what respect does your daughter look like you?" one cannot be asked, "In what respect do the lines look unequal in length?"

If we do not mean that the lines in the Muller-Lyer figure resemble unequal lines, and the green patch against a yellow background resembles a blue patch, what do we mean? The essential point, I suggest, is that the Muller-Lyer lines, and the green patch, look to me as I *would* judge them to be *if* it did not occur to me that I might be the subject of an illusion. Contrast this with the case of the resemblance use of "looks." My daughter looks like me. But this does not mean that she looks as I would judge her to be if it did not occur to me that I might be the subject of an illusion. I know what it would be to judge two lines to be unequal. What would it be to judge my daughter to be myself? The element of "would-be judgment" does not come into the resemblance case, and resemblance does not come into the "would-be judgment" case.

The upshot is that there is a distinction to be drawn not only between Anscombe's case in which the huntsman's father looked like a stag and cases in which something can look like an *X* without being taken to be an *X*, but also, within the latter class, between cases

like the Muller-Lyer lines looking unequal (i.e., cases
in which the "look" is identified by reference to what
I have called a "would-be judgment"), and those like
my daughter looking like me (i.e., resemblance cases).
But it is the former distinction which I want to empha-
size here. (I shall be returning to the latter distinction
in Chapter 3.) In *some* cases, then, O looks like an *X*
to S without S's taking O to be an *X*. That this is so in
some cases means that the generalization "Whenever
O looks like an *X* to S, S judges O to be an *X*" is false.
It is not universally true that being appeared to is judgment mediated by sensation (38, 264A).

There is a use of the word "looks" (or "appears")
which is different from both the "would-be judgment"
and resemblance uses.

It is sometimes said that a coin or a round plate looks
round only if seen head-on. Viewed from an angle, the
coin looks elliptical, the round plate like an oval one.
If normal vision were two-dimensional perhaps round
plates would look like oval ones in the sense in which
the wheel on the cinema screen appears to be revolving
—that is, so that if one did not know better, one would
take oneself to be seeing an oval plate, the sort used
under sauceboats. To people with normal vision, round
plates viewed at an angle do not usually look like oval
ones in that sense of "looks like." What, then, is the
sense in which they do look oval?

It is a matter of the observer's point of view relative
to the object and of the laws of perspective. If, like

someone setting out to draw a perspective-true picture of the plate, as it appears to a given point of view, one holds a pencil at arm's length, at right angles to one's line of vision, between one's eyes and the plate, and "measures" the plate latitudinally and longitudinally, the latitudinal measurement will be greater than the longitudinal one. More simply, if one put a transparent screen at right angles to one's line of vision, between oneself and the plate, and drew on it the outline of the plate seen through the screen, the shape drawn would be oval.

I shall call this measurable, objectively determined appearance of an object its "optical" appearance.

One can explain some illusions, but not others, by reference to the optical appearance. A straight staff, half immersed at an angle in water, looks, from many points of view, as if it were bent or broken at the water level. If one drew the outline of the staff on a transparent screen one would draw a bent or broken line. But in the case of the Muller-Lyer illusion, the lines one drew on the screen would be equal in length. If we wanted a terminology to mark the difference, we might say that the Muller-Lyer illusion was a visual illusion but not an optical one, whereas the bent-staff illusion was an optical one.

Psychological experiments (50) have shown that unless one uses pencils, screens, and so on, one is likely, in judging what the optical appearance is, to err on the side of the shape the object looks like in the sense in which a round plate looks like a round plate regardless of one's angle of vision. One cannot tell, just by looking at something, whether or not an illusion is an optical one. Take the case of the so-called "moon illusion." The moon looks larger when it is near the horizon than when it is directly overhead. Is this because the optical appearance is larger—perhaps because when it is near the horizon it is seen through more of the earth's atmosphere and this has a magnifying effect? One can be sure that the optical appearance is not larger only by measuring it. Our field of vision does not come with a built-in grid for measuring optical appearances.

One can be mistaken about a thing's optical appearance but can one be mistaken about what it looks like to one in the sense in which his father looked like a stag to the huntsman, or the Muller-Lyer lines look unequal to all of us? If O's looking like an X to S were a matter of S's noticing the resemblance of O to Xs, then, I suppose, S could be said to be mistaken. The resemblance he claimed to see might not exist. But O's looking like an X to S is not always a matter of noticing the resemblance of O to Xs, as we have seen.

Often, when one says "O looked like an X to S," one is unprepared to give a categorical "Yes" or "No" to the question "Do you mean S noticed some resemblance (which he could proceed to specify) O has to Xs?" Perhaps because of this indeterminacy of one's meaning and the possibility of being mistaken in the resemblance-noticing cases, one may feel that there are no cases in which it makes no sense to talk of a person being mistaken about what something looks like to him.

If we say of the huntsman to whom his father looked like a stag that he was mistaken, we mean, not that he was mistaken about his father looking to him like a stag, but that his belief that he was looking at a stag was a false belief. He was not wrong (or right) about his father appearing to him to be a stag. That his father looked to him like a stag was a fact, and facts, unlike beliefs, cannot be said to be true or false. I do not mean that we must restrict "true" and "false" to beliefs. If we allow ourselves to talk of *the look* (a stag) of his father, to the huntsman, this may be said to be false, in that what looked like a stag was not in fact a stag. Appearance did not reflect reality. The would-be judgment that identifies the look did not correspond to the facts.

In the case of the Muller-Lyer illusion, if someone knew it to be an illusion, there would be a false look but a true belief.

There is a danger in talking of his father looking like a stag to the huntsman as "the look" (a stag) of his father, to the huntsman. It suggests that, just as there can be a representation of the optical appearance (e.g., a picture) at which we could look, so there could be a representation of "the look" (e.g., a real stag) at which we could look. But if anything is a representation of his father looking to the huntsman like a stag it would be the huntsman aiming at his father, etc.

Another way of putting this is in terms of the distinction between "true to" and "true of." J. L. Austin writes:

> If, as some also say, a belief is 'of the nature of a picture', then it is of the nature of what cannot be true, though it may be, for example, faithful. . . . A picture, a copy, a replica, a photograph—these are *never* true in so far as they are reproductions, produced by natural or mechanical means: a reproduction can be accurate or lifelike (true *to* the original), as a gramophone recording or a transcription may be, but not true (of) as a record of proceedings can be. In the same way a (natural) sign *of* something can be infallible or unreliable but only an (artificial) sign *for* something can be right or wrong (5).

In terms of this distinction between "true to" and "true of," a representation (such as an image on the retina) of the optical appearance of an object can be said to be *true to* the optical appearance of the object. That is, given particulars about the lens of the eye, etc., one could correlate the retinal image and the optical appearance. But this is *quite* a different matter from S's belief that he is looking at a stag, or the look itself, being false. The belief, and the look, are false *of* what is in the undergrowth. They are false as propositions, not as pictures, are false. I shall mark this feature that the look shares with the belief, and does not share with a representation of the optical appearance, by calling the look the "epistemic" appearance. Perception would not be how we find things out about the world if there were not epistemic appearances. Or, in plain language, it is only because we see things as being things of a certain sort that we find out about the world by seeing things.

2

EXTENDING THE CAUSAL CHAIN
BEYOND THE BRAIN

Where, if anywhere, is the argument of the preceding chapter leading us? Let us recapitulate.

Were there not such a thing as seeing something *as* a thing of a certain kind (i.e., were there not what I have called "epistemic appearances"), there would not be perception as a way of coming to know things about the world. Sometimes, as in the case of the huntsman to whom his father looked like a stag, a person takes what he sees to be what it looks like; but this is not universally so. As in the case of the Muller-Lyer illusion, something can look X without one's judging it to be X. But to say this is not to deny that there is a relation between the epistemic appearance and a judgment: what a thing looks like to somebody is what he would judge it to be if he had no reason to think otherwise. To talk of "what a thing looks like" in this sense is not simply to talk of a resemblance that has been noticed. The huntsman did not shoot his father because he noticed a resemblance. In general, unless things could look like Xs in some sense other than that of resembling Xs they could not resemble Xs. Resemblance is a consequential property. And to talk of "what a thing looks like," in the sense of an epistemic appearance, is not to talk of its optical appearance. The optical appearance of an object to a point of view can be calculated by reference to its position vis-a-vis the object, and the laws of perspective. It can be said to be true *to* the object, in the sense of *representing* it according to a certain projection. The same can be said of the stimulation of the sense-organs (understanding "projection" more widely) and of the resulting state of excitation of the brain. These are effects of the object acting on the sense-organs. The epistemic appearance, on the other hand, is not something that can be correlated with the object as a projection or representation of it. It is true, or false, *of* the object.

This suggests a question, and a possible answer. What is essential to the concept of perception as a way of coming to know about the world is the concept of an epistemic appearance. The relationship between optical appearances and the world is a causal one. What is the relationship between epistemic appearances and the world? Is it, also, causal?

All that has been said, so far, about the relationship between epistemic appearances and the world is that an epistemic appearance can be identified by reference to what one's judgment would be (a "would-be judgment") about the world, if one made a judgment on the basis of how things appeared to one, and if one had no reason to judge things to be otherwise than as they appeared. This does not enable one, given that the object looked at is an X, to say what the epistemic appearance will be for an observer. This last, it might seem, is what we want, a statement of the relationship

between the world and epistemic appearances such that
from truths about the world we can derive truths about
its epistemic appearance.

From truths about the world we can certainly derive
truths about its optical appearance. Given the dimen-
sions of an object and its spatial relation to a point of
view, one can say what the optical appearance of the
object to that point of view is. It is determined, causally, by the laws of perspective. The stimulation of the
sense-organs of an observer occupying that point of
view, and the resulting state of excitation of his brain,
are similarly determined: causally. That is, given information about the object, the state of the observer
and the relevant causal laws, one could, in theory, determine what the state of excitation of the observer's
brain would be. Can one in the same, causal way determine the epistemic appearance of an object to an
observer?

Someone might say that this amounts to the question,
"Do things cause us to see them?" But these words
can be understood in a way such that the answer is, obviously, "No." The word "see" is often used so that if
S sees X but sees it as a Y, he is still said to see X, although he does not realize that it is an X. In this use of
"sees," it is a logical, and so not a causal, truth that if
something is an X and is seen by S, then S sees X.

Our question might be reworded as follows. An X
may look like an X or like a Y. That something *is* an

X explains its being seen as an X. But is it a *causal* explanation?

A. R. White would say that it was *not* a causal explanation. He writes:

> There are reasons why an X should sometimes look like an X and why it should sometimes look like a Y; the former reasons include a reference to X but they are not causal; the latter reasons are causal but include no reference to X (57).

What are the "former reasons"? White writes:

> I want to hold that the *explanation* of its looking to him as if there were a stick when he sees a stick is that he sees what he sees in normal conditions, and it is an analytically true statement that a stick looks to normal persons in normal conditions as if it were a stick.

D. W. Hamlyn would agree that the reasons why an X normally looks like an X are not causal, but not with White's alternative account in terms of analyticity. He says (16) that "it is not a contingent matter, not just an ordinary matter of fact, that, normally, we see things as they are," and "that there is, in some respects at least, an essential or internal connection between perception and how things are." Later, he says, "I have sought to show that there is some kind of necessity about the proposition that normally we see things in many respects as they are . . . but I do *not* think that the principle with which I have been concerned is logically necessary or *analytic*. There is nothing logically necessary in the proposition that we normally see red things as red."

White's reason for saying that the principle *is* analytically true is, "If *X* can look to anyone as if it were an *X,* then having a characteristic appearance is, I think, part of its being what it is."

What must we understand by this, if it is to yield the conclusion that "it is an analytically true statement that a stick looks to normal persons in normal conditions as if it were a stick"? Presumably, White means that part of what we *mean* by calling something a stick is that it looks like a stick to normal observers under normal conditions. Is *the rest* of what we mean that it feels, sounds, etc., like a stick, and behaves causally like a stick in relation to other things? If so, then perhaps if we restrict *X* to a proper object of the sense of sight, White would say that (the whole of) what we mean by calling something, say, red is that it looks red to normal persons in normal conditions.

Hamlyn says that "to say that something is red *cannot* be to say that it looks red under normal conditions." His argument is as follows:

Presumably someone could understand what it is for something to *look* red only if he already knew what it is for something to *be* red. Thus, to say that 'is red' *means* 'looks red under normal conditions' involves on the face of it a curious view of meaning, since the meaning of one expression is given in terms of another which itself appears intelligible only in terms of the first; the meaning of 'is red' is given in terms of 'looks red', but the latter could be understood only if 'is red' is already understood.

Hamlyn's rejection of White's view that the principle is analytically true leaves us with the question, "What then does he mean by saying that 'there is some kind of necessity about the proposition that normally we see things in many respects as they are'?" *What* kind of necessity?

Hamlyn's answer to this is that the "connection between the way people see coloured objects and what colours those objects actually have . . . lies in our concepts."

Before examining this answer—I shall in fact not return to it until the final chapter—let us reconsider the rejection of the causal explanation of red things looking red in normal conditions.

We have talked as if causal questions about perception could concern only the optical appearance, stimulation of the sense-organs, and excitation of the brain. Were we right so to do? Or can we somehow take the causal story beyond the excitation of the brain, in the hope of explaining perception, as an epistemic concept, in terms of causation and judgment, without invoking the concept of the epistemic appearance?

Descartes tried to do just this. He said that there are two distinct substances, non-extended thinking mind and extended non-thinking matter. Minds are intimately connected with those portions of matter which are people's brains; they have their "seat" in the head. In perception, the causal chain does not end with the excitation of the brain; the excitation of the brain "impresses" on the mind something variously called an "idea" or "sensation." (To avoid confusion with more familiar uses of these terms I shall call it a "sense-impression.") To each different brain state, resulting from different stimulations of the sense-organs, there corresponds a different sense-impression. The sense-impression is a modification of the mind, that is, of the non-extended thinking substance, but it is not a thought, and, in the case of visual perception, it is extended. Not being a thought, a work of the intellect, it cannot be said to be true or false. But with the sense-impression may come (1) a thought about it and (2) a thought about the external object that causes it. Any thought about it that occurs, being based on it, will be true to it. A thought about its cause (that is, the thought that the external object is, or is not, like the sense-impression in some respect), on the other hand, may be true or false. It comes naturally to us to think that the cause is like the sense-impression. We may realize on reflection that this is probably not the case, at least in respect of features like color. The initial, unreflective thought gives way to a more considered judgment, and may do so so rapidly that we are not conscious of having had it.

It is interesting to see how, in terms of this theory, Descartes deals with illusions. He considers the broken staff illusion and the moon illusion but not, to the best of my knowledge, the Muller-Lyer illusion.

His explanation of the broken staff illusion is in Section 9 of his reply to the Sixth Set of *Objections to the Meditations* (12, Vol. II, pp. 252–53). He refers here to the sense-impression as the "second grade of sense-perception" (the first grade is what he calls the "cerebral motion"). In the first and second grade of sense-perception, he says, "no falsity can reside." He goes on, "When, therefore, it is alleged that refraction makes a staff appear broken in the water, it is the same as if it were said that it appears to us in the same way as it would to an infant who judged that it was broken, and as it does even to us who, owing to the prejudices to which we from our earliest years have grown accustomed, judge in the same way." In other words, to say that a staff appears broken to us is to say that, on the basis of the image of the staff in the sense-impression being as it is, we make an unreflective judgment that we are looking at a broken staff.

His treatment of the moon illusion is more complicated. This is in the Sixth Discourse of the *Dioptric* (13, p. 179). He writes:

> The moon and the sun . . . usually appear to us as of only one or two feet in diameter at most, notwithstanding that, as we are sufficiently assured by our reason,

they are extremely large and extremely far distant. This
is not due to any fault in our power to conceive them
larger than we do; we can very well conceive towers
and mountains very much larger; but because, not being able to conceive them as farther removed from us
than a hundred or two hundred feet, it follows that
their diameter should not appear more than that of one
or two feet. Their situation also contributes to deceive
us in this regard; for ordinarily heavenly bodies seem
smaller when they are very high towards midday than
when, on rising and setting, diverse objects intervene between them and our eyes and so cause us to take better
notice of their distance. Astronomers, in measuring them
with their instruments, definitely prove that their appearing larger in the one situation than in the other is not
due to their being seen under a larger angle, but because they are judged to be more distant. And thus it
follows that the axiom of the ancient optics, which de-
clares that the apparent magnitude of objects is propor-
tioned to that of the angle of vision, is not always true.

"The axiom of the ancient optics" could, of course,
be saved if by "the apparent magnitude" we understood
"the optical appearance." It is the epistemic appearance, however, with which Descartes is here concerned.
And what he says is that the horizontal moon's looking
bigger is to be analyzed as the unreflective judgment
that it is bigger, which judgment is based on the reflection that the image of the moon in the sense-impression
is the same size although the moon is farther away.

To what lengths would Descartes have to go to explain away the Muller-Lyer illusion in terms of sense-

impressions and judgments? Of course, he might abandon the attempt to provide an analysis of the lines looking unequal like that he gives of the horizontal moon looking larger, and simply say that the lines in the sense-impression are unequal. But to do this would raise suspicions about his theory, for it might then seem that the character of the sense-impression was being read off from the epistemic appearance rather than that the epistemic appearance was being analyzed in terms of a "sense-impression" (the effect on the mind of a certain "cerebral motion") plus judgments based on it. If his theory is to be taken seriously, as involving an extension of the causal chain beyond the brain, he must avoid this suspicion at all costs.

It may be thought that the problem of how to accommodate non-optical illusions is a minor one for Descartes, compared to that of dealing with the following three objections to his theory. (1) The sense-impression is said to be a modification of a non-extended substance, the essence of which is thought, and yet *is* extended, and is *unlike* a thought in that it is not true or false of anything. (2) To say that the thought about the sense-impression is "based" on it is not to explain the relationship between the thought and the sense-impression. (3) No account is given of the relation between having the sense-impression and thinking that there is a cause of it external to the mind.

I shall say a little about the first of these objections

in this chapter, then discuss the second and third at greater length in Chapters 3 and 4 respectively.

What would have been Descartes's answer to the first of these objections?

In his reply to Princess Elizabeth's comment that she "could more readily allow that the soul has matter and extension than that an immaterial being has the capacity of moving a body and being affected by it" he invites her to feel free to ascribe matter and extension to the soul, provided she distinguishes between an extension which "is determined to a certain place, and excludes any other corporeal extension from that place" and an extension of which this is not true. The latter is the sort of extension that may be ascribed to the soul.

Can we apply this notion, of an extension which is not determined to a certain place and does not exclude any other corporeal extension from that place, to perception so as to understand how a sense-impression can be extended and yet not corporeal?

It is precisely because the sense-impression is unlike a thought, in that it is not true or false of anything, that there is a difficulty. If to talk of a "sense-impression" were to talk of a thought or an epistemic appearance, there would be no problem. Saying that someone thinks something is square, or that something looks square to him, is compatible with there being nothing square. There can be no conflict between "intentional" extension and corporeal extension. But Descartes's "ideas" had not this intentional character. Spinoza had Descartes in mind when he wrote:

> Those who think that ideas consist of images which are formed in us by the concourse of bodies . . . regard ideas as lifeless pictures on a board, and preoccupied thus with this misconception they do not see that an idea, in so far as it is an idea, involves affirmation or negation (46, Bk. II, Prop. XLIX).

Somehow the sense-impression has to be like a picture, literally extended, and yet non-corporeal, so that it does not exclude corporeal extensions.

I think the requirement can be met only be introducing some other concept besides that of extension and that of thought. I shall call this concept that of "the private," as opposed to "the public," using these terms in a way which is derived from, but not the same as, their ordinary use. An example may make this use clear. After looking at an electric light bulb, if I look at a blank wall it may look to me as if there is a dark patch on the wall. This is what is called an "afterimage." Its presence on the wall is compatible with the wall being blank. It is private to me. Sense-impressions are extended but, being private, they do not conflict with public extensions. They are, we might say, not in the same logical space as things like walls and brains. Descartes's visual sense-impressions can be thought of as, like pictures, extended but, unlike the pictures we hang on walls, private. By making the essence of the mind, not thinking (meaning, by "thinking," what can be true or false of something), but privacy, the seeming contradiction of something being a modification of the mind, and yet extended, can be avoided.

3

THE PRIVATE LANGUAGE THEORY

In the preceding chapter I asked, "What is the relationship between epistemic appearances and the world? Is it causal?" I noted that A. R. White and D. W. Hamlyn hold the relationship to be, in some sense, necessary. White holds it to be necessary in an analytic sense; Hamlyn sees difficulties in this view and says that the "connection between the way people see coloured objects and what colours those objects actually have . . . lies in our concepts." I postponed examining this answer to consider Descartes's attempt to explain perception in terms of a "sense-impression" caused in the mind by something happening in the brain, and judgments based on it. After touching on the problems of explaining illusions, especially non-optical ones, in terms of this theory, I considered an objection to the theory, an objection which can, I think, be met by introducing the notion of "the private." It is in virtue of its "privacy" that the sense-impression, although extended, is not corporeal.

In this chapter I shall consider the objection to Descartes's theory, that to say that the thought about the sense-impression is "based" on it is not to explain the relationship between the thought and the sense-impression.

There are no more than the barest hints of a reply to

this objection in Descartes's works. One can find more than hints in Locke. But it is not until we come to John Stuart Mill that we have the full flower of what I shall call "the private language theory."

Mill is concerned with the question "What does it mean to say that something is white?" He uses the term "sensation" for what Descartes calls a "sensation" or an "idea" and what I have called a "sense-impression." Making use of quotations from Mill, the argument of Book I, Chapter III, Sections 3, 4, 7, and 9 of his *System of Logic* (1843) may be summarized as follows:

On Descartes's representative theory of perception, something's looking white to us consists in our having sensations of white which are excited in us by the object. We attribute the quality, whiteness, to the object in virtue of its exciting the sensations. Moreover, "we know not, and cannot know, anything of bodies but the sensations which they excite in us." It follows that "those sensations must be all that we can, at bottom, mean by their attributes; and the distinction which we verbally make between the properties of things and the sensations we receive from them, must originate in the convenience of discourse rather than in the nature of what is signified by the terms." However, "it may be said that . . . because one thing may be the sole evidence of the existence of another thing, it does not follow that the two are one and the same. The attribute whiteness (it may be said) is not the fact of receiving the sensation, but something in the object itself; a *power* inherent in it; something *in virtue* of which the object produces the sensation." But the only foundation for this view is "the disposition, wherever we meet with two names which are not precisely synonymous, to suppose that they must be the names of two different things." The reasonable conclusion is that one and the same thing is "called a sensation when considered merely in itself, and a quality when looked at in relation to any one of the numerous objects, the presence of which to our organs excites in our minds that among various other sensations or feelings."

The last sentence of this repays careful study, especially the phrase "that among various other sensations or feelings." Mill means, "that *sensation* among various other sensations or feelings"; and "that sensation" is something of which it makes sense to say that numerous objects can excite it in our minds by their presence to our organs. But how can *numerous* objects excite *the same* sensation? Must not numerous objects excite *different,* though possibly exactly similar, sensations? Insofar as sensations are "things excited in our minds" they have the character of particulars; but insofar as a sensation can be excited by *numerous* objects, to talk of "a sensation of white" is to talk of something that can be said about any number of things. It is to talk of something "looking or being white," where "white" is a general word standing for a universal. Mill seems to be of two minds as to whether the "sensations" to which he refers have the character of particulars or universals.

We can see how he resolves the issue if we turn to

his editorial footnote (on pp. 260–61) to his father's *Analysis of the Phenomena of the Human Mind* (1869). James Mill in the text writes that it is "obvious, and certain, that men were led to class solely for the purpose of economizing in the use of names."

> Could the processes of naming and discourse have been as conveniently managed by a name for every individual, the names of classes, and the idea of classification, would never have existed. But as the limits of the human memory did not enable men to retain beyond a very limited number of names; and even if it had, as it would have required a most inconvenient portion of time, to run over in discourse, as many names of individuals, and of individual qualities, as there is occasion to refer to in discourse, it was necessary to have contrivances of abridgment.

In his footnote John Stuart Mill objects that economizing in the use of names is not the sole purpose of classification: "We could not have dispensed with names to mark the points in which different individuals resemble one another: and these are class-names." In other words, we need class-names to predicate qualities of individuals.

From the passage quoted from James Mill it might seem that he would reply that names can be given to "individual qualities" without classification; that is, that names of "individual qualities" are not class-names.

John Stuart Mill notices this (he quotes the sentence in question, italicizing "and of individual qualities"), and proceeds (i) to ask what is meant by an "individual quality," (ii) as if he knows the answer to this question (namely, the individual qualities of an object are "the individual and instantaneous impressions which it produces in us"), to deny that predicating a quality of an object is predicating of it one of its individual qualities, and (iii) to say what it is to predicate a quality of an object (namely, "to assert that the object affects us in a manner similar to that in which we are affected by a known class of objects"). He writes:

But what is meant by an individual quality? It is not *individual* qualities that we ever have occasion to predicate. It is true that the qualities of an object are only the various ways in which we or other minds are affected by it, and these affections are not the same in different objects, except in the sense in which the word same stands for exact similarity. But we never have occasion to predicate of an object the individual and instantaneous impressions which it produces in us. The only meaning of predicating a quality at all, is to affirm a resemblance. When we ascribe a quality to an object we intend to assert that the object affects us in a manner similar to that in which we are affected by a known class of objects. A quality, indeed, in the custom of language, does not admit of individuality: it is supposed to be one thing common to many; which, being explained, means that it is the name of a resemblance among our sensations, and not a name of the individual sensations which resemble. Qualities, therefore, cannot be predicated without general names; nor, consequently, without classification.

In this passage Mill resolutely turns his back on allowing sensations to have a universal character. "These affections are not the same in different objects, except in the sense in which the word same stands for exact similarity." This being so, he has to locate the universality elsewhere. He locates it in the resemblance of a sensation to other sensations. He holds what in Chapter 1 I called "the resemblance doctrine."

Mill's version of the resemblance doctrine, however, differs from that of some other, more recent, holders of it—and not merely in that for him it is a matter of the resemblance of sensations, not objects.

His version can be introduced by asking, "What is classification?" To find out whether an element is a metal, a metal being defined as an element whose oxide dissolved in water yields an alkaline solution, I have to find out whether the element has this peculiarity in common with other metals. Is this process of finding out (performing tests indicated by the definition) classification? Or is only pronouncing the element to be a metal (or a non-metal) classification? The point is that not all general names have definitions. The names for what Mill calls "simple feelings" have not. Consequently, there is no test I can perform, comparable to dissolving oxides in water, etc., to give me the right to say something looks white. All I can do is to look. Things do not look white in virtue of something analytically involved in their looking white, something which they have in common—as metals have in common that their oxides dissolved in water yield an alkaline solution—with other things that look white (Cf. 32). If we say that they do have something in common with other things that look white we must remember that *their having something in common simply is their looking white*. It makes sense to say, "Ah, now I see what metals have in common"; but it makes no sense to say, "Ah, now I see what things that look white have in common." They do not look white in virtue of having something in common; they have something in common (their whiteness) in virtue of looking white. Their resemblance is a consequence, not a precondition, of their looking white.

There are several ways in which this difference between names like "metal" and those like "white" can be marked. One would be to say that the predicating of names like "white" does not involve classification (taking classification to be the performing of tests indicated by the definition of the general name). Another would be to say that whereas some classes (e.g., the class *metal*) are grounded on resemblance in some respect, others (e.g., the class *sensation of white*) are not grounded on resemblance at all. (This is not to deny that the members of the class resemble one another—they must—but only that the resemblance comes first, and so can be the "ground" of the class.) To say this would be to deny the universality of what Ayer says it is natural for us to assume, namely that we use the same word in different situations because we have noticed a distinctive common feature.

Mill adopts neither of these ways of marking the difference. He marks it by distinguishing between resemblance in a given particular, resemblance which consists in the possession of certain common peculiarities, on the one hand, and what he calls "mere general resemblance," "general unanalysable resemblance," or "simple likeness," on the other. Sensations of white are not alike in some respect; they are alike "altogether." In his *System of Logic* (Bk. I, Chapter V, Section 6) he writes:

It is sometimes said, that all propositions whatever, of which the predicate is a general name, do, in point of fact, affirm or deny resemblance. . . . There is some slight degree of foundation for this remark, but no more than a slight degree. The arrangement of things into classes, such as the class *metal,* or the class *man,* is grounded indeed on a resemblance among the things which are placed in the same class, but not on a mere general resemblance; the resemblance it is grounded on consists in the possession by all those things of certain common peculiarities; and those peculiarities it is which the terms connote, and which the propositions consequently assert; not the resemblance. For though when I say Gold is a metal, I say by implication that if there be any other metals it must resemble them, yet if there were no other metals I might still assert the proposition with the same meaning as at present, namely that gold has the various properties implied in the word metal. . . . Propositions, therefore, in which objects are re-

ferred to a class, because they possess the attributes con-
stituting the class, are so far from asserting nothing but
resemblance, that they do not properly speaking, assert
resemblance at all. . . . [There is an] exceptional case,
in which, though the predicate is the name of a class, yet
in predicating it we affirm nothing but resemblance, the
class being founded not on resemblance in any given
particular, but on general unanalysable resemblance.
The classes in question are those into which our simple
sensations, or rather simple feelings, are divided. Sensations of white, for instance, are classed together, not because we can take them to pieces, and say they are alike
in this, and not alike in that, but because we feel them
to be alike altogether, though in different degrees. When,
therefore, I say The colour I saw yesterday was a white
colour, or, The sensation I feel is one of tightness, in
both cases the attribute I affirm of the colour or of the
other sensation is mere resemblance—simple *likeness* to
sensations I have had before, and which have had those
names bestowed upon them. The names of feelings, like
other concrete general names, are connotative; but they
connote a mere resemblance. When predicated of any
individual feeling, the information they convey is that
of its likeness to the other feelings which we have been
accustomed to call by the same name.

To understand this we have to see that Mill is basing
his answer to one question on his answer to another.
There is the question "Why do we use the same color-
word in different situations?" to which Mill gives the
answer "Not because of resemblance in some respect,
but because of *mere* resemblance"; and there is the
question "What does the color-word connote?" to

which Mill gives the answer "The mere resemblance." He is stuck with this answer to the second question because he holds that what one is saying about something when one calls it X is identical with one's reason for calling it X.

In short, his argument is of the form:

1. Sensations of white are not alike in *some respect;* they are alike *altogether.*

Therefore,

2. My reason for calling a sensation "a sensation of white" is not its resemblance *in some respect* to other sensations called by the same name, but its *mere* resemblance to them.

But

3. What I *mean* by calling a sensation "a sensation of white" is the same as my *reason* for calling it "a sensation of white."

Therefore,

4. What I *mean* by calling a sensation "a sensation of white" is its *mere* resemblance to other sensations called by the same name.

In the footnote to *Analysis of the Phenomena of the Human Mind,* Mill says that it is not "the individual and instantaneous impressions" that an object produces in us that we predicate of the object. How does he conceive of these "impressions"?

In Book I, Chapter III, Section 3 of his *System of Logic* (written before he had decided that a quality is simply a sensation regarded in a certain relation) he distinguishes between a sensation and a quality, a distinction which, he feels, may be missed because we can seldom refer to the sensation otherwise than by a circumlocution, e.g., by reference to the quality as when we call a sensation "the sensation of white." This suggests that he thinks of the impression as being something that *could* have a name of its own. He regrets that "language, which adapts itself for the most part only to the common uses of life, has provided us with no single-worded or immediate designation" for the impression. This suggestion is combined with his version of the resemblance doctrine in the following passage from Book I, Chapter VIII, Section 2:

> The only names which are unsusceptible of definition, because their meaning is unsusceptible of analysis, are the names of the simple feelings themselves. These are in the same condition as proper names. They are not indeed, like proper names, unmeaning; for the words sensation of white signify, that the sensation which I so denominate resembles other sensations which I remember to have had before, and to have called by that name. But as we have no words by which to recall those former sensations except the very word which we seek to define, or some other which, being exactly synonymous with it, requires definition as such, words cannot unfold the signification of this class of names; and we are obliged to make a direct appeal to the personal experience of the individual whom we address.

The implication of this passage is that the words

"sensation of white" *denote* the particular sensation under consideration, but *connote* its resemblance to other sensations called by the same name. The words "sensation of white" are *unlike* a proper name in that they have connotation. They differ from connotative terms like "metal"—and to this extent "are in the same condition as proper names"—in that the signification of "white" cannot be unfolded. That is, whereas to the question "What are the things the resemblance to which you mark by calling this thing a 'metal'?" the answer "Things of which it is true that their oxide dissolved in water yields an alkaline solution" can be given, no such answer can be given to the question "What are the things the resemblance to which you mark by calling this sensation 'a sensation of white'?" To this question the only answer that can be given is, "Sensations to which I have given the name 'sensation of white,'" and this is an answer that does not "unfold the signification of this class of names." The signification is private to the user, and he can only hope that resemblances in his own experience have their counterpart in the experience of others, so that they can attach a meaning of their own to what he says.

But this is not all. It is not just that when *I* call something "white" I am saying that my sensation resembles an earlier sensation of *mine,* and that when *you* call something "white" you are saying that your sensation resembles an earlier sensation of *yours,* so that when I tell you that something is white I rely, for your under-

standing anything by what I say, on there being a resemblance among the sensations in your experience
corresponding to that among mine. As if this were not
bad enough, there is the further implication that the
resemblance is unspecifiable, is only a "simple likeness." Nothing can be said about the respect in which
my, or your, earlier and later sensations resemble one
another. To say that they are alike in respect of whiteness would be like saying that I call them by the same
name because I call them by the same name. This is
because, on the view in question, "in respect of whiteness" means no more than "in respect of being like my
earlier sensations." It is not just that there is no public
rule for the application of "white"; there is no private
rule, either. The attempt to base a connotation on a
denotation plus a "simple" resemblance cannot but fail.
That is not how descriptive language works.

4

THE HIGH ROAD TO PHENOMENALISM

In Chapter 2 I listed three objections to the account of perception which involves extending the causal chain beyond the brain. The first objection—that the sense-impression is said to be a modification of a non-extended substance the essence of which is thought, and yet *is* extended and is *unlike* a thought in that it is not true or false of anything—was met by making the essence of mind privacy, not thought.

The second objection was that to say that the thought about the sense-impression is "based" on it is not to explain the relationship between the thought and the sense-impression. In Chapter 3 I examined an account of the meaning of words like "white" which explains this relationship, but which at the same time, I claim, makes the use of "white" as a descriptive word impossible.

The third objection, to be considered in this chapter, was that no account is given of the relationship between having the sense-impression and thinking that there is a cause of it external to the mind.

Descartes did, in fact, give an account of this relationship. Perhaps it can best be understood if we consider, first, the views of John Locke and George Berkeley.

John Locke (29, Bk. IV, Ch. XXIII, Sect. 5) advanced an argument which may be formulated as follows:

(a) All the ideas a person has are produced either by the person himself or by material things outside him.
(b) The only ideas a person produces himself are ones he produces at his pleasure, as, for example, when he recalls the idea of light.
(c) Some ideas a person has are not produced at his pleasure.
Therefore,
(d) Some ideas a person has are produced by material things outside him.

Two possible objections to the first premise of this argument are (i) that something other than the person himself or material things outside him may produce a person's ideas, and (ii) that it does not follow from a person having ideas that there is a thing that produces them. With regard to the first of these objections it might, for instance, be held that a person's ideas are produced by a non-material agent, or agents, other than the person who has them.

A theory along these lines was held by George Berkeley. Having rejected the Lockean notion of matter, he concluded, from a premise similar to Locke's, about some of a person's ideas not being ones he produces at his pleasure, that they are produced by "some other will or spirit," namely God (10, Sect. 29).

Descartes had in fact considered a view rather like

that of Berkeley, and rejected it. His argument, in the Third and Sixth of the *Meditations on First Philosophy*, as it applies to Berkeley's view, may be formulated as follows:

(1) I am given ideas of sensible objects.

(2) I could not be given them were there not something, either myself or something else, that produces them in me.

(3) Since production of the ideas does not depend on my intellect, and the ideas are produced without my co-operation, and often against my will, *I* do not produce them.

Therefore,

(4) Something else produces them.

(5) This "something else" may be as we are strongly inclined to think of it, namely corporeal, or it may be God.

(6) God would be deceitful if he produced ideas himself and gave me both a strong inclination to believe that they proceed from corporeal objects and no means of establishing their true origin.

But,

(7) God, being liable to no defects, is not deceitful.

Therefore,

(8) Ideas proceed from corporeal objects.

But will this do? In (6) above, Descartes seems to be admitting not only (a) that we have a strong inclination to believe that our ideas proceed from corporeal objects, but also (b) that we have no means of establishing their true origin. Another way of expressing (b) would be to say that there are no observations we could make which would establish, or tend to establish, the truth of what we believe. In other words, the sentence "Ideas proceed from corporeal objects" does not mean anything to us in terms of any conceivable verifying experience. But what, then, does it mean?

> The criterion which we use to test the genuineness of apparent statements of fact is the criterion of verifiability. We say that a sentence is factually significant to any given person, if, and only if, he knows how to verify the proposition which it purports to express—that is, if he knows what observations would lead him, under certain conditions, to accept the proposition as being true, or reject it as being false. If, on the other hand, the putative proposition is of such a character that the assumption of its truth, or falsehood, is consistent with any assumption whatsoever concerning the nature of his future experience, then, as far as he is concerned, it is, if not a tautology, a mere pseudo-proposition. The sentence expressing it may be emotionally significant to him; but it is not literally significant.

So wrote A. J. Ayer (7, p. 35).

Can the "factual significance" of "Ideas proceed from corporeal objects" be saved without sacrificing the verifiability principle of meaning? Only, it might be thought, by accepting a phenomenalist analysis of "Ideas proceed from corporeal objects." What I mean by this may be introduced by reference to Berkeley, again.

In Section 29 of the *Principles* he writes:

When in broad day-light I open my eyes, it is not in my power to choose whether I shall see or no, or to determine what particular objects shall present themselves to my view; and so likewise as to the hearing and other senses, the ideas imprinted on them are not creatures of my will. (There is *therefore some other will or spirit* that *produces them.*)

Then in the next section he writes:

(The ideas of sense are more strong, lively, and *distinct* than those of the imagination; they have likewise a steadiness, order, and coherence, and are not excited at random, as those which are the effects of human wills often are, but in a regular train or series, the admirable connection whereof sufficiently testifies the wisdom and benevolence of its Author.) Now *the set rules or established methods wherein the Mind we depend on excites in us the ideas of sense, are called the laws of nature:* and these we learn by experience, which teaches us that such and such ideas are attended with such and such other ideas, in the ordinary course of things.

In the course of arguing that those ideas we have which are not dependent on our own wills are dependent on God's will, Berkeley provides us with a means of distinguishing between the two kinds of idea, a

means which does not involve a reference to something
that transcends our experience. "Ideas of sense," as
he calls them, are ideas which are attended with other
ideas in a regular train or series. But if there is this
means of distinguishing between the two kinds of idea,
what need have we of *either* Locke's (and Descartes's)
material substance *or* Berkeley's "other will or spirit"?
If the answer to this question is "No need," then we
have, in effect, chosen to define reality in terms of ideas,
ideas which connect up with other ideas in certain ways,
ways which we call "the laws of nature."

But another answer is possible, namely that we *do*
need something besides a means of distinguishing between the two kinds of idea, we need some equivalent,
in our idea-l-ism, to what is implicit in the physical
object language, that physical objects do not cease to
exist when we close our eyes.

This is another job that is carried out by God, in
Berkeley's theory. In Section 45 of the *Principles* he
states the following objection to his view that the things
we perceive by sense (houses, mountains, rivers, etc.)
are nothing but our ideas or sensations:

> The objects of sense exist only when they are perceived:
> the trees therefore are in the garden, or the chairs in
> the parlour, no longer than while there is somebody by
> to perceive them. Upon *shutting my eyes,* all the furni-
> ture in the room is reduced to nothing, and barely upon
> opening them it is again created.

To this objection he replied, in Section 48:

> (. . . though we hold, indeed, the objects of sense to be nothing else but ideas which cannot exist unperceived, yet we may not hence conclude they have no existence, except only while they are perceived by *us*, since *there may be some other spirit that perceives them, though we do not*). . . . It does not therefore follow from the foregoing principles, that bodies are annihilated and created every moment, or exist not at all during the intervals between our perception of them.

It is, of course, this objection and reply that have been immortalized in the limericks:

> There was a young man who said "God
> Must think it exceedingly odd
>   If he finds that this tree
>   Continues to be
> When there's no-one about in the quad."

and

> Dear Sir, *your* astonishment's odd.
> *I* am always about in the quad
>   And that's why the tree
>   Will continue to be
> Since observed by,
>   Yours faithfully,
>   God

In some passages in Berkeley there are, however, the seeds of a different answer, one which involves neither material substance nor God. In Section 3 of the *Principles*, for example, he writes,

> The table I write on, I say, exists, that is, I see and feel it; and if I were out of my study I should say it existed, meaning thereby that if I was in my study I might perceive it, or that some other spirit actually does perceive it.

The significant phrase is, "meaning thereby that if I was in my study I might perceive it." What is suggested by this phrase is an analysis of statements about physical objects into not just statements about *actual* ideas or sensations but also statements about *possible* ideas or sensations—ideas or sensations one would have *if* one put oneself in a position to have them. Such an analysis makes reference to nothing other than ideas or sensations, and so seems to provide a meaning for physical object statements to which a holder of the verifiability principle of meaning could raise no objection. Such an analysis is what is known as "phenomenalism." It is stated explicitly by John Stuart Mill.

> Matter, then, may be defined, a Permanent Possibility of Sensation. If I am asked, whether I believe in matter, I ask whether the questioner accepts this definition of it. If he does, I believe in matter: and so do all Berkeleians. In any other sense than this, I do not. But I affirm with confidence, that this conception of matter includes the whole meaning attached to it by the common

world, apart from philosophical, and sometimes from theological, theories.

Now, not everything that is implicit in the physical object language can be represented in a phenomenalist analysis. Consider the following two statements.

(a) Someone who believed the proposition "All actual and possible sensations are such as to confirm the existence of a table in my study" would have every reason to disbelieve, and no reason to believe, the proposition "There is not a table in my study."

(b) The propositions "All actual and possible sensations are such as to confirm the existence of a table in my study" and "There is not a table in my study" are logically incompatible.

It is very easy to slip from believing (a), which is *not* an expression of phenomenalism, to believing (b), which *is* an expression of phenomenalism. The falsity of (b), but not of (a), is implicit in the physical object language. If (b) were true then physical objects would not be what, by definition, they are, namely objects that exist independently of actual or possible experiences of them.

The ease of slipping from believing (a) to believing (b) may be illustrated by reference to what Ayer, who rarely makes slips like this, says in *The Problem of Knowledge,* Ch. 3. Having devoted a whole section to arguing that "the phenomenalist's programme cannot be carried through" and having remarked that the assumption "that since statements about physical objects can be verified or falsified only through the occurrence of sense-data, they must somehow be reducible to sense-data" is false, he writes, in the next section:

. . . Suppose it were the case that in what appeared to be the relevant setting the object would always seem to be perceived, no matter what further experiences were obtainable. Then, I think, it would logically follow that the object did exist. . . . [If the premise] were true in any given instance, the existence of a certain physical object would, on the evidence, be logically guaranteed.

This is phenomenalism.

5

ARE THERE PHYSICAL OBJECTS?

The road I traced to phenomenalism in the previous chapter is not the only road. There are other starting points besides that of the Cartesian sense-impression. One such is that of the "sense-datum" as it has been introduced in various ways by G. E. Moore, H. H. Price, and others.

The question of whether acceptance of some version of the verifiability principle commits one to phenomenalism is one that can be raised independently of questions about sense-impressions, sense-data, etc. In this chapter I shall advance a view which is, I think, non-phenomenalistic, and yet is in sympathy with some version of the verifiability principle.

A book often, rightly, recommended to newcomers to philosophy is Bertrand Russell's *Problems of Philosophy*. A question is raised in the first two chapters, "Do things other than ourselves and our experiences exist?" and it is suggested (a) that we instinctively believe, or unthinkingly assume, that there is "an independent external world," and (b) that what we instinctively believe may be questioned. In Chapter Two Russell refers to "the common-sense hypothesis that there really are objects independent of us." He is looking for a justification for the belief, or assumption, or hypothesis.

When the terms "belief," "assumption," and "hypothesis" are used in this context, is their use the ordinary one? Is the "justification" for which the philosopher searches what we ordinarily mean by "justification"?

The words "Are there physical objects?" may ask two different questions. The first is what I shall call "a question *within* the realm of physical objects"; the second, "a question *about* the realm of physical objects." I shall try to show that, in the ordinary sense of "assumption," it would be absurd to say that in answering either of these questions in the affirmative we are making an assumption. If it is absurd to say that we are making an assumption, then it is equally absurd to say that we are making a justified, or an unjustified, assumption.

A question within the realm of physical objects

Some philosophers have sometimes treated the words "Are there physical objects?" as if they asked a question within the realm of physical objects, that is, a question about what is in the world in the way in which "Is there a sheet of paper in the drawer?" and "Are there unicorns nowadays?" are questions about what is in the world.

For example, J. McT. E. McTaggart, in *Some Dogmas of Religion*, questioned "the possibility of matter existing independently of spirit," and concluded his reflections with, "The result is that matter is in the same position as the Gorgons or the Harpies. Its existence is a bare possibility to which it would be foolish to attach the least importance, since there is nothing to make it at all preferable to any other hypothesis."

W. T. Stace, in an article entitled "The Refutation of Realism," discussed the proposition that some entities sometimes exist without being experienced. He came to the conclusion, "It will follow that the realistic position that they do exist is perfectly groundless and gratuitous, and one which ought not to be believed. It will be in exactly the same position as the proposition 'there is a unicorn on the planet Mars.' I cannot prove that there is no unicorn on Mars. But since there is not the slightest reason to suppose that there is one, it is a proposition which ought not to be believed."

And G. E. Moore, in his "Proof of an External World," concluded, firstly, that to prove that there are objects external to our minds it is sufficient to show that there are, for example, soap-bubbles, sheets of paper, hands, shoes, and socks, and secondly, that one can show this by, for example, holding up a hand and saying, "Here is a hand." It was this article which he began with a quotation from Kant's *Critique of Pure Reason,* "It still remains a scandal to philosophy . . . that the existence of things outside of us . . . must be accepted merely on faith, and that, if anyone thinks good to doubt their existence, we are unable to counter his doubts by any satisfactory proof."

The things which McTaggart, Stace, and Moore say in these passages have this in common; just as one can conceive a hand, so one can conceive Gorgons and Harpies, and even a unicorn on Mars. One can imagine the sort of circumstances which would lead astronomers or space explorers to say, "Now we know there are (or are not) unicorns on Mars." So if the words "Are there physical objects?" ask a question like the questions "Are there Gorgons or Harpies?" "Is there a unicorn on Mars?" and "Is there a hand here?" they ask a question which we know how to go about answering. In these passages McTaggart, Stace, and Moore are all treating the words "Are there physical objects?" as though they asked a question to the answering of which would be appropriate the procedures appropriate to answering a question about a member of the class of physical objects, for example, "Is there a hand here?," "Is there a unicorn on Mars?" They are all treating the words "Are there physical objects?" as though they asked a question *within* the realm of physical objects.

Now, if this is the question which is being asked, then Moore's answer is clearly the correct one. In answering the question otherwise than as Moore does, McTaggart and Stace show that they have confused it with some other question. A person cannot be consistent in saying, as Stace does, both that the proposition "Some entities sometimes exist without being experienced" is in the same position as the proposition

"There is a unicorn on the planet Mars," and also that "there is no possible way in which we could know" that any single entity exists unexperienced. For there is a possible, a conceivable, way in which we could know whether there is or is not a unicorn on Mars. Nor can a person be consistent in saying, as McTaggart does, both that "matter is in the same position as the Gorgons or the Harpies" and also that "the independent existence and ultimate nature of matter is a question for metaphysics and not for science." For the question of whether there are Gorgons or Harpies is a question for science, in the sense of being a question we answer by examining the world.

If the words "There are physical objects" are to be understood as expressing an empirical proposition like "There are cats" and "There are unicorns," then to say it is a proposition we only assume to be true implies that it is unlike these propositions in being something we believe without the sort of justification we have for believing "There are cats," or for disbelieving "There are unicorns." Saying it is a proposition we assume to be true implies that it is like "Whatever you read in the newspapers is true," which is something some people do assume. But if it is an empirical proposition, then its truth follows from the truth of *any* such proposition as "There are cats" or "Here is a hand," which are things it would be absurd to say we only assume.

We know what it would be for a physical object not

to exist when not perceived. If the floor of a room in which a person was sitting no longer existed when he closed his eyes, he and his chair would fall through into the room below. We can thus imagine one thing ceasing to exist when nobody is looking at it, and the havoc and amazement it would cause. In point of fact we know of nothing which does cease to exist when unperceived. And so the answer to the empirical question "Are there things which can exist unexperienced?" is "Yes, of course."

The categories of matter, causation, and time are conceptually linked. At any moment in time a physical object is the effect of its previous states and the cause of its subsequent ones. Consequently, to ask for an answer to the question "Are there things which can exist unperceived?" which does not depend on causal evidence would be like asking for an answer to the question "How long have we been here?" which does not make use of evidence to the effect that certain things (the position of clock hands, etc.) have changed. Only the admission of such evidence gives the words "Are there things which can exist unperceived?" a meaning. If one excludes the use of such evidence, it is not that one is asking a question to which there is no answer—one is not asking a question at all.

A question about the realm of physical objects

In deciding what sort of procedure is appropriate to answering a question, we automatically decide what sort of a question it is. If the procedure by which we answer the question "Are there physical objects?" is that by which we ordinarily answer such a question as "Is there a table in the room?", then it is a straightforward existential question. And the answer to it is "Yes, of course," this answer to be accompanied by a puzzled frown and the feeling that the inquirer cannot have asked what he meant to ask. If the procedure by which we answer the question is not this, then it does not ask a question about what is in the world, it does not ask a question within the realm of physical objects.

I propose now to try to give a meaning to the words "Are there physical objects?" so that they ask, not a question *within* the realm of physical objects, but a question *about* the realm of physical objects.

To this end I must first distinguish two kinds of statement. The distinction is based on what I said in Chapter 1 about epistemic appearances, and is the distinction between a report by someone on what something looks like to him, in the "epistemic appearance" sense of "looks like," and a claim he makes, on the basis of what it looks like to him, as to what it is. I implied in Chapter 1 that it makes no sense to talk of a person being mistaken about what something looks like to him in the "epistemic appearance" sense. Only insofar as, in saying that something looks like an *X,* one is describing its optical appearance, or claiming that it resembles an *X,* does it make sense to talk of being mistaken.

I shall refer to this feature of epistemic appearance statements as their "mistake-meaninglessness." To say that they are mistake-proof, even to say that they are categorically mistake-proof, or "incorrigible," would be misleading; it would mislead some people into thinking that, whereas it makes no sense to talk of a person being *wrong* about what something looks like to him, it not only does make sense to talk of his being *right* about what it looks like to him, but moreover he cannot but be right. My point is that the question "Is he right or wrong?" does not apply when someone reports an epistemic appearance.

In the way in which epistemic appearance statements are mistake-meaningless, the claims a person makes on the basis of what something looks like to him are not mistake-meaningless. I shall call such claims "reality statements."

A second feature of epistemic appearance statements, in which they differ from reality statements, is that they might be said to be about objects—"the looks" of things—that are *not* "independent of us." They might be said to be about our experiences.

I said, they *might* be said to be about objects that

are not independent of us, or about our experiences.
In Chapter 1 I warned against talking of his father
looking to the huntsman like a stag as "the look" (a
stag) of his father, to the huntsman, saying that it suggests that just as there can be a representation of the
optical appearance (e.g., a picture) at which we could
look, so there could be a representation of "the look"
(e.g., a real stag) at which we could look. I said that
if anything is a representation of his father looking to
the huntsman like a stag it would be the huntsman
aiming at his father, etc. A related warning about saying that epistemic appearance statements are about objects that are not independent of us, or about our experiences, would be that saying either of these things
suggests that such statements can be understood independently of reality statements being understood. If it
is said that epistemic appearance statements are about
objects that are not independent of us, or about our
experiences, it must not be inferred that what they are
about is independent of what is independent of us.
Why? Because when I say, for example, that the lines
in the Muller-Lyer figure look unequal what I mean is
that they look to me as I would judge them to be if it
did not occur to me that I might be the subject of an
illusion. Epistemic appearances are identified by reference to what I called "would-be judgments," and the
judgments in question are expressed in reality statements. Epistemic appearance statements might be said
to be conceptually parasitic on reality statements. But

this is not incompatible with their categorical subjectivity. Epistemic appearances are appearances *to us.* If there were no beings to whom things appeared there could be no epistemic appearances.

We have, then, a class of statements, epistemic appearance statements, which are mistake-meaningless and subjective, and a class of statements, reality statements, which are not mistake-meaningless and not subjective. How are they related?

In Chapter 1 I said that an epistemic appearance, unlike an optical appearance, can be said to be true or false *of* the world. This, added to the mistake-meaninglessness of epistemic appearance statements, means that if a certain mistake-meaningless statement is true, then one or other of two non-mistake-meaningless statements is true, the mistake-meaningless statement being one about how things appear, and the non-mistake-meaningless ones being to the effect that things are, or are not, as they appear. For the most part we know very well how to decide whether or not things are as they appear. Certain very general elements in this "knowledge-how" can be formulated in "knowledge-that" statements. As such they are logical truths of the physical object language. An example would be, "*X* being a quality that can be apprehended by more than one sense (such as roundness, apprehended by sight and touch), other things being equal, the judgment based on something's looking *X*, that it is *X*, is confirmed by its feeling *X*."

The meaning I propose for the words "Are there physical objects?" so that they ask a question *about* the realm of physical objects is this: "Do we use this language, with these logical truths relating how things appear and how things are?" The answer, of course, is, "Yes, of course we do."

Except, as now, when we are philosophizing, we do not formulate the knowledge-how in knowledge-that statements. It might be said that we "unthinkingly know" the logical truths of the physical object language. But to pass from saying this to saying that we "unthinkingly assume" or "instinctively believe" there are physical objects would be to confuse the question about the realm of physical objects with the question within the realm. The two questions would similarly be confused if one objected to an affirmative answer to the question about the realm, "But in that case if we stopped using this language, with these logical truths, then physical objects would cease to exist, and that is absurd." (Compare this with the objection to a verbalistic account of necessary truth which confuses a question about a realm with one within a realm, "But 2 plus 2 would still equal 4 even if nobody used '2 plus 2' and '4' interchangeably again.")

Confirmation and Verification

I promised to advance a view which is non-phenomenalistic and yet in sympathy with some version of the verifiability principle. How is what I have said saved from being phenomenalistic? In two ways, depending on what one takes phenomenalism to be.

(1) It is saved from one sort of phenomenalism by my not identifying the questions within, and about, the realm of physical objects.

(2) It is saved from another—the more usual—sort by (a) my taking, as the things to be related, epistemic appearance statements and reality statements, the former of which are, as I put it, "conceptually parasitic on the latter," and (b) my using the word "confirm," rather than the word "verify," in the example of a logical truth of the physical object language relating how things appear to how things are. To confirm a proposition is to establish it more firmly, whereas to verify it is to establish its truth.

If something feels, as well as looks, round, that establishes more firmly that it is round; it does not exclude, once and for all, the possibility that it is not round. It would do this only if "It is round" *meant* "It looks and feels round," only, that is, if reality statements were reducible to epistemic appearance statements. This view that they are so reducible is phenomenalism.

It is of some interest to note that the verifiability principle, in some of its formulations, would appear to be a confirmability principle. One such formulation is that given by Ayer, quoted in Chapter 4. Observations which lead someone to accept a proposition as being true are not the same as observations which entail the truth of a proposition. One can be led to accept as being true, even be justified in believing, a proposition which is, in fact, false.

Two grounds for asserting a conceptual connection

I have said that epistemic appearance statements might be said to be conceptually parasitic on reality statements. The ground I gave for this remark was that epistemic appearances are identified by reference to what I called "would-be judgments," and the judgments in question are expressed in reality statements. In other words, "It looks red" and "Its looks are such that I would judge it to be red if I had no reason to judge otherwise" have, with certain qualifications, the same meaning.

A different ground for saying that epistemic appearance statements are conceptually parasitic on reality statements is to be found in reflections on how we might have learned to use epistemic appearance statements.

Wittgenstein, in *Zettel*, 422, asks, "Why doesn't one teach a child the language-game 'It looks red to me' from the start? Because it is not yet able to understand the rather fine distinction between seeming and being?" In Section 418 he had written, "To begin by teaching someone 'That looks red' makes no sense. For he must say that spontaneously once he has learnt what 'red'

means, i.e. has learnt the technique of using the word."
Learning the technique of using a word is, for Wittgenstein, a matter of being trained to react as the rest of us do to certain things (things which we can specify only by using the word in question). This agreement in reaction is not agreement in opinion; the concept of it does not enter into the language game (*Zettel,* 430); it is a prerequisite of agreement, or disagreement, in opinion. That such agreement underlies the working of the language game is likely to be overlooked until one comes up against a disagreement which it is difficult to regard as one of opinion. (Remember the story of the small boy who asked why his French visitor called something a shoe when it was obviously a cabbage.) If the necessity for the agreement is overlooked, then so will be the necessity of the child's being trained to react to certain things in a certain way for it to mean anything by "It is red." And so it may seem that a child, without having learned the technique of using the word "red," might *start* by learning "That looks red to me."

I shall be making use of this notion of a conceptual connection grounded in a language-learning situation in the next chapter.

6

A CONCEPTUAL CONNECTION

It is time, once again, to recapitulate.

In Chapter 1 I distinguished three senses of "looks like" or "appears," which I called the "resemblance" sense, the "optical" sense, and the "epistemic" sense. I was concerned primarily to establish the distinctness, and importance, of the third of these senses.

With regard to the distinctness of the epistemic sense, (1) I argued that the epistemic sense could not be analyzed in terms of the resemblance sense since something must look like an X in a non-resemblance sense if anything is to look like an X in a resemblance sense. That two things look alike to someone is a *consequence* of their both having, or appearing to have, the same property. (2) I said that the epistemic sense differs from the optical sense in that whereas a representation of the optical appearance can be true or false *to* the world, only the epistemic appearance can share with propositions the property of being true or false *of* the world.

With regard to the importance of the epistemic sense I said that perception would not be how we find things out about the world if there were not epistemic appearances; it is only because we see things as being things of a certain sort that we find things out about the world by seeing things.

In Chapter 2 I raised the following question:

Representations of the optical appearance, such as a certain state of excitation of the brain, are effects of an object acting on the sense-organs. The relationship between such representations of optical appearances, and the world, is thus a causal one. Is the relationship between epistemic appearances and the world causal, also? That something *is* an X explains its being seen as an X. Is it a causal explanation?

Perhaps a belated word of warning is in place here. The question of whether something's being an X *causally* explains its being seen as an X might unreasonably be confused with the much wider question of whether causal concepts have any place at all in the analysis of the concept of seeing. To this wider question the answer, of course, is that they do have a place. We would not say, without qualification, that someone saw something if the sense-organs for sight, the eyes, were not stimulated. We would say, perhaps, that he was suffering from a hallucination; or if, without his eyes being stimulated, he could report faithfully on what was in the world, that it was an instance of extrasensory perception. In this way, causal concepts are built into our concept of seeing, though it is left to scientists to discover the details of "the physical basis of perception." The question is not whether there are causal conditions of an object's being seen (it is part of our concept of seeing, that there are), but whether the explanation, that an object *is* an *X,* of its being seen as an *X* is a causal explanation.

An analogy may help. In distinguishing between knowing and believing, philosophers often say that it is a condition of someone's knowing some proposition, *p,* that *p* is true. It can then be asked whether this is a causal or some other kind of condition. If it were decided that it was not a causal condition, it would not follow that knowing did not have causal conditions such as that the knower's brain is undamaged. (The analogy must not be taken too far, however. It is not a necessary condition of something's being seen as an *X* that it *is* an *X.*)

I return, now, to the recapitulation.

In Chapter 2 I went on to consider A. R. White's view that "it is an analytically true statement that a stick looks to normal persons in normal conditions as if it were a stick." I gave D. W. Hamlyn's objection to this view, as it applies to redness, namely that "to say that 'is red' *means* 'looks red under normal conditions' involves on the face of it a curious view of meaning since the meaning of one expression is given in terms of another which itself appears intelligible only in terms of the first." I postponed examination of Hamlyn's own view that the "connection between the way people see coloured objects and what colours those objects actually have . . . lies in our concepts" until this, the final, chapter. I did so in order to consider the Cartesian attempt to explain perception as an epistemic concept, in terms of causation and judgment. Descartes thinks of the causal chain (light reflected from the object—stimulation of the retinae—impulses in the optic nerves—excitation of the brain) being extended into something non-physical, the mind, so as to produce there something called an "idea" or "sensation," which is accompanied by a thought about it, based on it, and a thought about the external object that causes it.

Apart from the difficulties of accommodating non-optical illusions such as the Muller-Lyer illusion within such a theory and of squaring the mind being non-physical with visual ideas being extended, there are two problems raised by the theory which have been the staple diet of epistemologists ever since. One is that of explaining how the thought about the "idea" (or "sense-impression," as I called it) is related to it. The other is that of explaining why there should be thoughts about external objects at all, if all we are aware of in perception are impressions on our minds.

I considered the first of these two problems in Chapter 3.

A view open to Descartes is that which was propounded by John Stuart Mill two hundred years later. Descartes could have said that the thought about the sense-impression—the application of a predicate to it—is "based" on the sense-impression in the sense that when the predicate-expression is first used it is in fact merely a *name* given to a sense-impression, and that it is used subsequently to mark the resemblance of other sense-impressions to the one to which the name was given.

Mill makes clear two paradoxical corollaries of this view.

(a) The resemblance I mark, between a later sense-impression and an earlier one, by calling the later one "a sensation of white," is a *simple* resemblance.

In other words, it is *not* a resemblance *in some specifiable respect*. I cannot informatively say that the later sense-impression resembles the earlier one "in respect of whiteness." I cannot say this because *all I mean* by "in respect of whiteness" is "in respect of resembling a sensation to which I gave the name 'sensation of whiteness.'" (To the question "In what respect is *Y* like *X*?" it is not an informative answer to say "In respect of resembling that to which the name '*X*' was given.")

In other words, it cannot make sense on this view to say that two sense-impressions resemble one another in that they both have the same property. Instead of resemblance depending on properties, properties are analyzed in terms of "simple" resemblances, a "simple" resemblance between two things being one which is not a consequence of the two things having some property in common.

(b) The second paradoxical corollary of this view is that since sense-impressions are private to the people who have them, when we tell others that something is white "we are obliged to make a direct appeal to the personal experience of the individual whom we address."

In other words, when *I* call something "white" I am saying that my sensations resemble an earlier sensation of *mine,* and when *you* call something "white" you are saying that your sensation resembles an earlier sensation of *yours.* And when I tell you that something is white I rely, for your understanding *anything* by what I say, on there being a "simple likeness" among the sensations in your experience corresponding to the simple likeness among the sensations in my experience.

It may be worth noting, in passing, that if the talk of "simple likeness" is taken seriously, Mill's view does not allow of the following problem: "Although we use the same words for the same things, since your sensations are inaccessible to me I can never be sure that what you call 'a sensation of white' I wouldn't call 'a sensation of red' if only they were accessible to me." Someone to whom this problem makes sense cannot have fully accepted the reduction of properties to resemblances.

In Chapter 4 I discussed the difficulty, for Descartes's theory, of explaining why there should be thoughts about external objects at all, if all we are aware of in perception are impressions on our minds. Descartes's own explanation involves a causal principle (there must be something that produces my ideas), a principle about myself (to yield the conclusion that *I* do not produce them), the proposition that we are strongly inclined to believe they are produced by material things, and a doctrine about God not allowing us to believe things that are not true without having some means of discovering them not to be true. If one accepts only half of the last element in his explanation, namely that we have not the means of confirming or disconfirming that the sources of our ideas are material things, then, as Kant saw, we cannot exclude the possibility that the sources are non-corporeal thinking beings. It is in the context of such unverifiable speculation and skepticism that phenomenalism seems attractive.

Descartes writes of our having a strong inclination to believe that ideas proceed from corporeal objects. Not very different is Bertrand Russell's saying that we instinctively believe that there are things other than ourselves and our experiences. Saying this presupposes that we know what question is being asked with the words "Are there things that exist independently of us and of our experiences ('physical objects')?" In Chapter 5 I distinguished two meanings for the words "Are there physical objects?" which I called "a question *within* the realm of physical objects" and "a question *about* the realm of physical objects." Giving an affirmative answer to the question within the realm of physical objects does not involve speculation, and skepticism with regard to an affirmative answer is absurd. Moore was right. We know how to distinguish between real things and hallucinated things, and phenomenalism is true only of the latter.

What has struck philosophers about answers to questions within the realm of physical objects is that it is always meaningful to say of someone that he is mistaken about, e.g., there being an ashtray on the table in front of him. Our use of the word "certain" is such that it might be ridiculous to say that someone is not certain about there being an ashtray, but to say this is not to deny a meaning to the words "He is mistaken." In this respect, "It is an ashtray" differs from "It looks like an ashtray" if the latter is my report of an epistemic appearance to me. Such "looks" can be said to be mistake-meaningless, and mind-dependent, in contrast to physical objects. If we restricted our utterances to reports of epistemic appearances and called them "the objects of our perception," there would be no place for "the argument from illusion" and its heirs. The words "Are there physical objects?" can be taken to mean "Do we not restrict our utterances in this way?" and as such they ask a question *about* the realm of physical objects.

But *could* we restrict our utterances to reports of epistemic appearances? I mentioned two reasons for saying that we could not. The first was that the epistemic appearance of an object to someone is identified by what he would judge the object to be had he no reason to think otherwise. The second was the Wittgensteinian "language-learning" one, that the language game in which one says, "It looks red to me," (the language game of "the red visual impression") can be acquired only if one has already mastered that in which one says, "It is red."

In this final chapter I return to the question of the "connection between the way people see coloured objects and what colours those objects actually have," a connection which Hamlyn says "lies in our concepts."

After rejecting the sort of connection (an analytic one) for which White argues, Hamlyn writes:

> But even if it is wrong to say that there is an identity of meaning between "is red" and "looks red under normal conditions", it does not follow that it is wrong to say that something is red if and only if it looks red under normal conditions (including in this a reference to normal observers). Given what I have already said, the argument for this conclusion might go as follows.
>
> To say that something is red is to say that the concept *red* is properly to be applied to it. It follows that if people have the concept *red,* in the full sense which implies an ability to recognise red things, then other things being equal, they should apply the concept in this case, i.e., that, other things being equal, they should see the thing in question as red. From this in turn it follows that there is justification for the ascription of redness to something *only if,* other things being equal, people see it as red—and other things will be equal only if conditions are normal.

To understand this argument I think one has to approach it with a certain question in mind, the question

"How is our having the concept *red* (our understanding anything by '. . . is [or is not] red') related to red things normally looking red to us?" What sort of considerations will provide us with an answer, or with a clue to a way of answering, this question? Consider the questions: "Would we say of someone confronted with red things under normal conditions, but who evidently did not realize that the concept *red* applied to them, that he had the concept *red?*" and "If someone realizes, simply from looking at something, that the concept *red* applies to it, is not this the same thing as his seeing it as red, i.e., its looking red to him (in the epistemic appearance sense of 'looking')?" If to the last two questions we give the answers "No" and "Yes" respectively, then we are well on the way to giving, to the earlier question, the answer, "If red things did not normally look red to us, then we could not be said to have the concept *red,* to understand anything by '. . . is (or is not) red'; so if 'Red things do not normally look red to us' were true, it would not be intelligible to us; its falsity is guaranteed by its intelligibility; in other words the truth of 'Red things normally look red to us' is involved in our having the concept *red;* it is necessarily true, not in the sense of being analytic ('is red' does not *mean* 'looks red under normal conditions'), but in the sense of having to be true to be intelligible; there is this conceptual, but not analytic, connection between being red and looking red under normal conditions."

Hamlyn's argument may be set out as follows,

(i) To say that something is red is to say that the concept *red* is properly to be applied to it.
Therefore,
(ii) If people have the concept *red*, in the full sense which implies an ability to recognize red things, then, other things being equal, they should apply the concept in this case, i.e., other things being equal, they should see the thing in question as red.
Therefore,
(iii) There is justification for the ascription of redness to something *only if*, other things being equal, people see it as red—and other things will be equal only if conditions are normal.

Approaching this argument with the question "How is our having the concept *red* related to red things normally looking red to us?" in mind, one might want to reword it, as follows:

(i, reworded) To say that a thing is red is to say that it is such that anyone with the concept *red*, confronted with the thing under normal conditions, would be right to apply the concept to it.
Therefore (from [i, reworded]),
(ii, reworded) If a thing is red, and if anyone has the concept *red* in the full sense (that is, in the sense which is such that we would deny he had the concept if he did not apply it to red things with which he was confronted under normal conditions) he would be right, if confronted with the thing under normal conditions, to apply the concept to the thing.

Therefore (from [i, reworded], and [ii, reworded]), (iii, reworded) There is justification for saying that a thing is red only if there is justification for saying that it is such that anyone who has the concept *red,* confronted with the thing under normal conditions, would apply the concept; and since there is justification for saying that anyone has the concept *red* only if he would normally apply it to red things, that is, only if red things normally look red to him, there is justification for saying that a thing is red only if red things normally look red to people.

Note that to say "There is justification *only if* . . ." is not the same thing as to say "There is justification *if* . . .". Hamlyn's next sentence, after the passage quoted above, is, "That there is reason for saying that something is red *if* people see it as such seems a more obvious point for which I shall not here argue. . . ."

Conclusion

There are different kinds of questions that can be asked about perception. Some are causal; some are conceptual. The history of the philosophy of perception over the last three hundred years or so has been the history of an attempt to give a causal, or a partly causal, answer to a conceptual question; of what that answer implies as to the meaning of statements like "The snow is white" and "There is an ashtray on the desk"; and of

the dawning realization, in fairly recent years, of the
mistake about the nature of the question.

A number of factors contributed to the mistake. The
main one was the Cartesian dualist account of our nature. If I, the real I, am not "one single person who has
at once body and consciousness" (Descartes's account
of the notion "which everybody always has in himself
without doing philosophy"), but am a non-corporeal
substance related to the corporeal world causally (via
a gland in "my" head), then any question about perception automatically becomes, in part at least, a causal
question. What I, as such a substance, am aware of can
only be an "impression" made on my substance by the
corporeal world; and (a) talk of what I see something
as (its epistemic appearance) has to be interpreted in
terms of a thought I have about this private sense-
impression, and (b) talk of the thing I see (a physical
object) has to be interpreted in terms of a supposed
cause of the impression.

Cartesian dualism was the main factor contributing
to the mistake, but the mistake was made easier by the
ambiguity of expressions like "looks like" and "appears." Granted that the laws of perspective are causal
laws, there are "looks" of things (their optical appearances) which are causally related to them. If the epistemic appearance is confused with the optical appearance it may then seem to make sense to talk of the
epistemic appearance as an effect, of something's looking like an X being explained *causally* by its being an X,

seen under normal conditions. And if the epistemic sense of "looks like" is confused with the resemblance sense the reduction of properties to resemblances may seem no reduction at all.

The task of the philosopher of perception is that of distinguishing the different kinds of questions that can be asked about perception, and answering the conceptual ones. The idea that his task is to "justify our claims to knowledge of the external world," or to "analyze perception" in terms of "sensations" ("sense-impressions," "sense-data," etc.) and judgments based on them, is itself the product of the mistake to prevent which he should have been working.

NOTES ON READING

Chapter 1

A great deal has been written on the different senses of "looks like" or "appear." In the text I say that what I call the "epistemic appearance" can be identified by reference to a "would-be judgment" (p. 9), and can be said to be true or false *of* the world (p. 14). This is substantially what I said in my "Seeing and Seeing As" (54). There is a good critical examination of part of this paper in K. Lycos (30).

N. R. Hanson (19) is useful on the distinction between the epistemic appearance and what I call the "optical appearance."

I think I owe my ideas on the resemblance doctrine mainly to what Wittgenstein says in the second part of the *Brown Book* (58). In general, Wittgenstein has had a profound influence on my thinking. I do not know of any short passage on perception to compare with Part II, Section xi, of his *Philosophical Investigations* (60). Whether I have understood him is another matter.

Chapter 2

On the "internal connection between perception and how things are," the discussion of which is started in this chapter and taken up again in Chapter 6, the most important paper is D. W. Hamlyn (16). A. R. White (57) should also be read.

On the different uses of "see," see P. Alexander (1). For the view that there are not different senses of "see," see J. L. Austin (4, Ch. 9).

Descartes's observations on perception are rather scattered. There is an all too short systematic treatment in Section 9 of his reply to the Sixth Set of *Objections to the Meditations*. The chapter on "Ideas" in A. Kenny, *Descartes: A Study of His Philosophy* (26) is to be recommended.

Chapter 3

What I say about J. S. Mill's version of the private language theory in this chapter is based on my paper "Sensations of Colour" (52).

The private language theory is often discussed in terms of bodily sensations, but I think that doing so can confuse the issue. Bodily sensations present special problems for communication, ones on which I have written in a book (53), and, more recently, in a paper (51).

Chapter 4

There are references to Locke, *Essay Concerning Human Understanding* (29); Berkeley, *Treatise Concerning the Principles of Human Knowledge* (10); and Mill, *An Examination of Sir W. Hamilton's Philosophy* (34) in the text of the chapter. By comparison with "the way of ideas" introduced by Descartes, I do not think that Locke, Berkeley, Hume, Mill, or, for that matter, Kant, introduce fundamentally new ideas. The crucial step is that of setting out to answer a conceptual question as if it were a causal one. Once that step is taken one is committed to "the high road to phenomenalism," and what bypaths one takes, or stops one makes, are a secondary matter.

Chapter 5

This chapter is a revised version of my paper "Unthinking Assumptions and Their Justification" (55). In part, the revision is to take account of things J. L. Austin says (4, pp. 111–13). The ideas in my paper are much more ably expressed in Wittgenstein (59).

Chapter 6

Apart from the recapitulation of the substance of previous chapters, with which this chapter begins, it is concerned entirely with D. W. Hamlyn, "Seeing Things as They Are" (16). An interesting paper, to compare with Hamlyn's, is D. M. Taylor (49).

General

The suggestions for reading made above refer mainly to ideas developed in the chapters of this book. For more general background reading I recommend D. M. Armstrong (3), A. J. Ayer (8, 9), R. M. Chisholm (11), F. I. Dretske (14), F. B. Ebersole (15), D. W. Hamlyn (17, 18), F. A. Hayek (21), R. J. Hirst (23), D. Locke (28), H. H. Price (39, 40), G. Ryle (43, 44), and J. F. Soltis (45). Three useful collections of papers on perception are those edited by R. J. Hirst (22), R. J. Swartz (48), and G. J. Warnock (56).

BIBLIOGRAPHY

(1) Alexander, P., "Inferences about Seeing," in *Royal Institute of Philosophy Lectures,* 3, 1968–69, *Knowledge and Necessity,* Macmillan, London, and St. Martin's Press, New York, 1970.

(2) Anscombe, G. E. M., "The Intentionality of Sensation: A Grammatical Feature," in Butler, R. J. (ed.), *Analytical Philosophy, Second Series,* Blackwell, Oxford, 1965; Barnes & Noble, New York.

(3) Armstrong, D. M., *Perception and the Physical World,* Routledge and Kegan Paul, London, 1961; Humanities Press, New York.

(4) Austin, J. L., *Sense and Sensibilia,* Clarendon Press, Oxford, 1962.

(5) Austin, J. L., "Truth," *P.A.S.S.,* XXIV, 1950.

(6) Ayer, A. J., "Basic Propositions," in Black, M. (ed.), *Philosophical Analysis,* Cornell University Press, Ithaca, New York, 1950.

(7) Ayer, A. J., *Language, Truth and Logic,* 2nd ed., V. Gollancz, London, 1946; Dover, New York.

(8) Ayer, A. J., *The Foundations of Empirical Knowledge,* Macmillan, London, 1940; St. Martin's, New York.

(9) Ayer, A. J., *The Problem of Knowledge,* Macmillan, London, 1956; Penguin Books, Baltimore, Maryland.

(10) Berkeley, G., *Treatise Concerning the Principles of Human Knowledge,* 1710.

(11) Chisholm, R. M., *Perceiving: A Philosophical Study,* Cornell University Press, Ithaca, New York, 1957.

(12)   Descartes, R., *Philosophical Works of Descartes*, tr. Haldane, E. S., and Ross, G. R. T., Cambridge University Press, Cambridge, 1911.

(13)   Descartes, R., *Philosophical Writings*, tr. Smith, N. K., Macmillan, London, 1952.

(14)   Dretske, F. I., *Seeing and Knowing*, Routledge and Kegan Paul, London, 1969; University of Chicago Press, Chicago, Illinois.

(15)   Ebersole, F. B., *Things We Know*, University of Oregon Books, Oregon, 1967.

(16)   Hamlyn, D. W., "Seeing Things as They Are," An inaugural lecture delivered at Birkbeck College, May 24, 1965.

(17)   Hamlyn, D. W., *Sensation and Perception*, Routledge and Kegan Paul, London, 1961; Humanities Press, New York.

(18)   Hamlyn, D. W., *The Psychology of Perception*, Routledge and Kegan Paul, London, 1956; Humanities Press, New York.

(19)   Hanson, N. R., "On Having the Same Visual Experiences," *Mind*, LXIX, 1960.

(20)   Hare, R. M., *Freedom and Reason*, Clarendon Press, Oxford, 1963.

(21)   Hayek, F. A., *The Sensory Order*, Routledge and Kegan Paul, London, 1952; University of Chicago Press, Chicago, Illinois.

(22)   Hirst, R. J. (ed.), *Perception and the External World*, Macmillan, New York, 1965.

(23)   Hirst, R. J., *The Problems of Perception*, Allen and Unwin, London, 1959; Humanities Press, New York.

(24)   Hume, D., *A Treatise of Human Nature*, 1739.

(25)   Kant, I., *Critique of Pure Reason*, 1781.

(26)   Kenny, A., *Descartes: A Study of his Philosophy*, Random House, New York, 1968.

(27)   Lazerowitz, M., "The Existence of Universals," *Mind*, LV, 1946.

(28)   Locke, D., *Perception and Our Knowledge of the External World*, Allen and Unwin, London, 1967; Humanities Press, New York.

(29) Locke, J., *Essay Concerning Human Understanding*, 1687.

(30) Lycos, K., "Aristotle and Plato on 'Appearing,'" *Mind*, LXXIII, 1964.

(31) McTaggart, J. McT. E., *Some Dogmas of Religion*, Edward Arnold, London, 1906; Greenwood Press, Westport, Connecticut, 1969.

(32) Manser, A., "Games and Family Resemblance," *Philosophy*, XLII, 1967.

(33) Mill, James, *Analysis of the Phenomena of the Human Mind*, 1869.

(34) Mill, J. S., *An Examination of Sir William Hamilton's Philosophy*, 1865.

(35) Mill, J. S., *System of Logic*, 1843.

(36) Moore, G. E., "Proof of an External World," *Proceedings of the British Academy*, 1939.

(37) Moore, E. G. *Some Main Problems of Philosophy*, Allen and Unwin, London, 1953; Collier-Macmillan, New York, 1962.

(38) Plato, *Sophist*.

(39) Price, H. H., *Perception*, Methuen, London, 1932; Dover Publications, New York, 1950.

(40) Price, H. H., *Thinking and Experience*, Hutchinson University Library, London, 1953.

(41) Reid, T., *Essays on the Intellectual Powers of Man*, 1785.

(42) Russell, B., *Problems of Philosophy*, Home University Library, London, 1912; Oxford University Press, Oxford, 1959.

(43) Ryle, G., *Concept of Mind*, Hutchinson University Library, London, 1949; Barnes & Noble, New York.

(44) Ryle, G., *Dilemmas*, Cambridge University Press, Cambridge, 1954.

(45) Soltis, J. F., *Seeing, Knowing and Believing*, Allen and Unwin, London, 1966; Addison-Wesley, Reading, Massachusetts.

(46) Spinoza, B., *Ethics*, 1677.

(47) Stace, W. T., "The Refutation of Realism," *Mind*, XLIII, 1934.

(48) Swartz, R. J. (ed.), *Perceiving, Sensing, and Knowing,* Doubleday, New York, 1965.

(49) Taylor, D. M., "The Incommunicability of Content," *Mind,* LXXV, 1966.

(50) Thouless, R. H., "Phenomenal Regression to the 'Real' Object," *British Journal of Psychology,* 21, 1931, 22, 1932.

(51) Vesey, G. N. A., "Being and Feeling," *P.A.S.,* LXIX, 1969.

(52) Vesey, G. N. A., "Sensations of Colour," in Schneewind, J. B. (ed.), *Mill,* Doubleday, New York, 1968.

(53) Vesey, G. N. A., *The Embodied Mind,* Allen and Unwin, London, 1965; Humanities Press, New York.

(54) Vesey, G. N. A., "Seeing and Seeing As," *P.A.S.,* LVI, 1956.

(55) Vesey, G. N. A., "Unthinking Assumptions and Their Justification," *Mind,* LXIII, 1954.

(56) Warnock, G. J. (ed.), *The Philosophy of Perception,* Oxford University Press, Oxford, 1967.

(57) White, A. R., "The Causal Theory of Perception," *P.A.S.S.,* XXXV, 1961.

(58) Wittgenstein, L., *Blue and Brown Books,* Blackwell, Oxford, 1958; Barnes & Noble, New York.

(59) Wittgenstein, L., *On Certainty,* Blackwell, Oxford, 1969; Harper and Row, New York.

(60) Wittgenstein, L., *Philosophical Investigations,* Blackwell, Oxford, 1953; Barnes & Noble, New York, 1964.

(61) Wittgenstein, L., *Zettel,* Blackwell, Oxford, 1967.

INDEX